Clarence P. Hornung

ALLOVER PATTERNS
for Designers
and Craftsmen

Dover Publications, Inc., New York

Allover Patterns for Designers and Craftsmen is a new work, first published by Dover Publications, Inc., in 1975.

DOVER *Pictorial Archive* SERIES

International Standard Book Number: 0-486-23179-8
Library of Congress Catalog Card Number: 75-13125

Manufactured in the United States of America
Dover Publications, Inc.
31 East 2nd Street
Mineola, N.Y. 11501

Introduction

In my *Handbook of Designs and Devices*, published in 1932, I attempted to provide a grammar of individual design elements, a compendium of forms to stimulate the creative imagination. The purpose of the present book is to extend the scope of my efforts to allover patterns. Such patterns are especially useful for many fabric, package and wallpaper designs because they repeat infinitely in all directions.

I have deliberately presented a wide variety in the 90 patterns: some are open and airy, others closely knit; some are rectilinear, others sinuous. There are geometrics and florals (natural and calligraphic), mazes, stippled patterns, "negatives," basketweaves, fanciful snowflakes, and three-dimensional designs that give the effect of cubes or receding coffers.

I have drawn upon both European and Oriental styles, from Greek meanders and Celtic spiral whorls to Arabic geometric stars and Chinese lattices. The largest single group is that inspired by the incredibly rich heritage of Japanese decorative art. These plates are largely derived from the centuries-old tradition of *mon,* or family crests. Among the Japanese design motifs represented are flowers, bamboo and reeds, birds and fish, stylized wave patterns, written characters, and the geometric forms kown as "tortoise shells," "scales" and "lightning."

The continued sales, for more than forty years, of the *Handbook of Designs and Devices* indicates that it has been a useful tool for artists and designers. I hope that *Allover Patterns* will also prove similarly helpful for as many years.

C. P. H.

PLATE 1

PLATE 2

PLATE 3

PLATE 4

PLATE 5

PLATE 6

PLATE 7

PLATE 8

PLATE 9

PLATE 10

PLATE 11

PLATE 12

PLATE 13

PLATE 14

PLATE 15

PLATE 16

PLATE 17

PLATE 18

PLATE 19

PLATE 20

PLATE 21

PLATE 22

PLATE 23

PLATE 24

PLATE 25

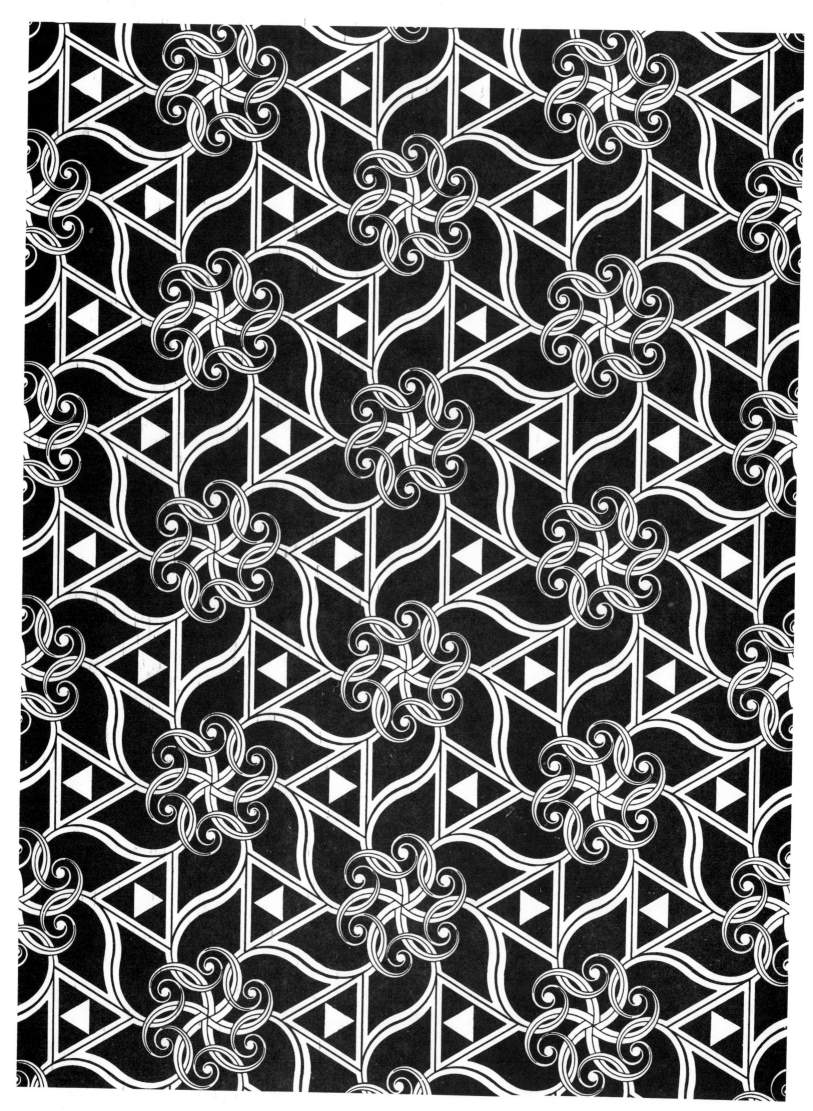

PLATE 26

PLATE 27

PLATE 28

PLATE 29

PLATE 30

PLATE 31

PLATE 32

PLATE 33

PLATE 34

PLATE 35

PLATE 36

PLATE 37

PLATE 38

PLATE 39

PLATE 40

PLATE 41

PLATE 42

PLATE 43

PLATE 44

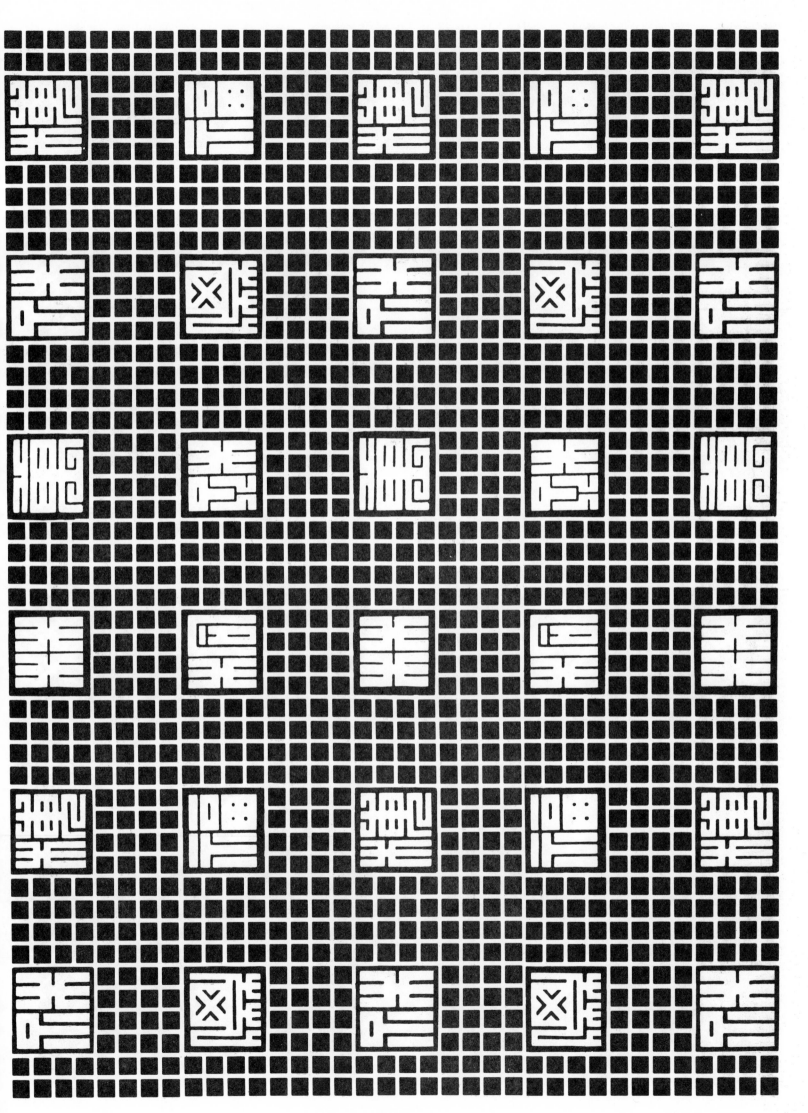

PLATE 45

PLATE 46

PLATE 47

PLATE 48

PLATE 49

PLATE 50

PLATE 51

PLATE 52

PLATE 53

PLATE 54

PLATE 55

PLATE 56

PLATE 57

PLATE 58

PLATE 59

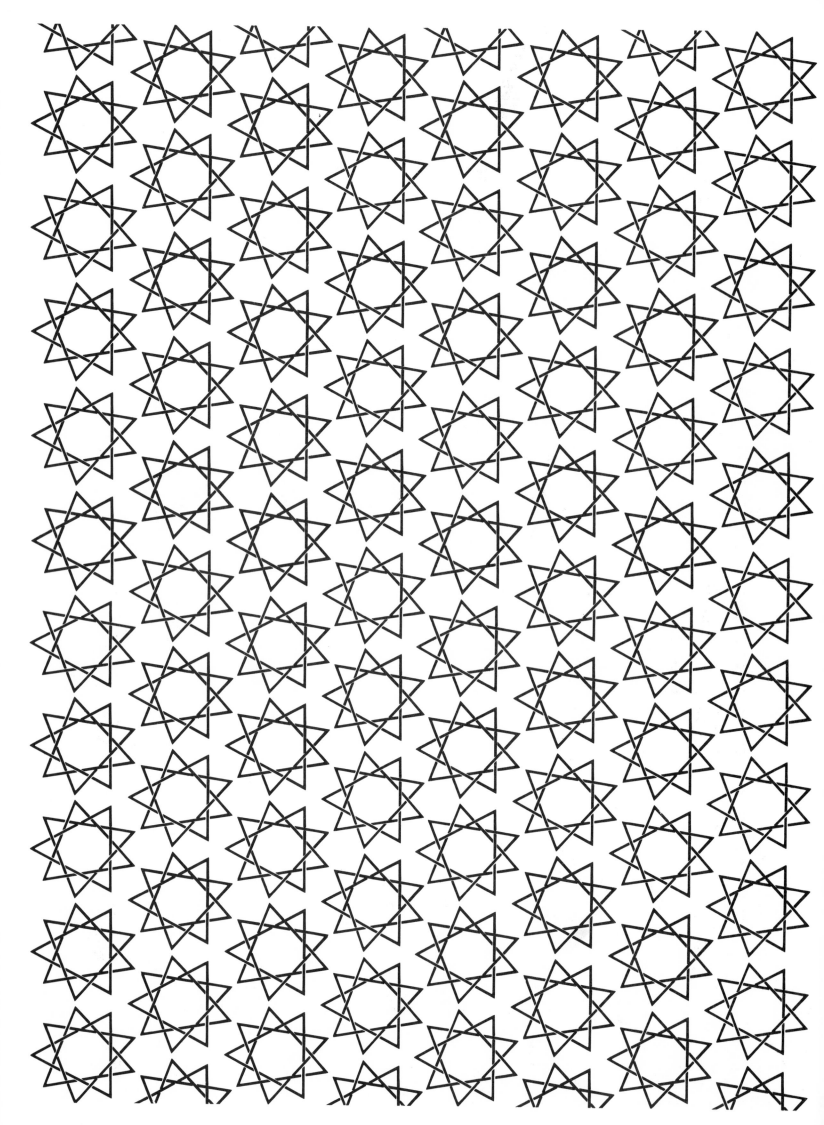

PLATE 60

PLATE 61

PLATE 62

PLATE 63

PLATE 64

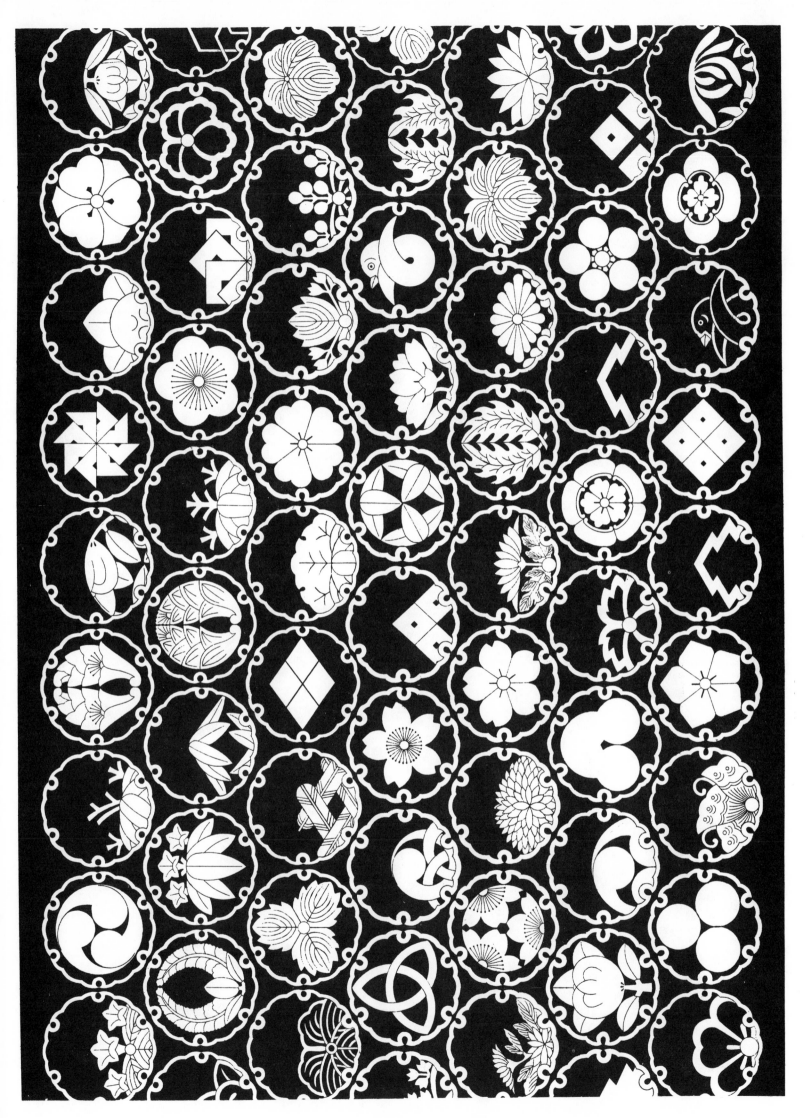

PLATE 65

PLATE 66

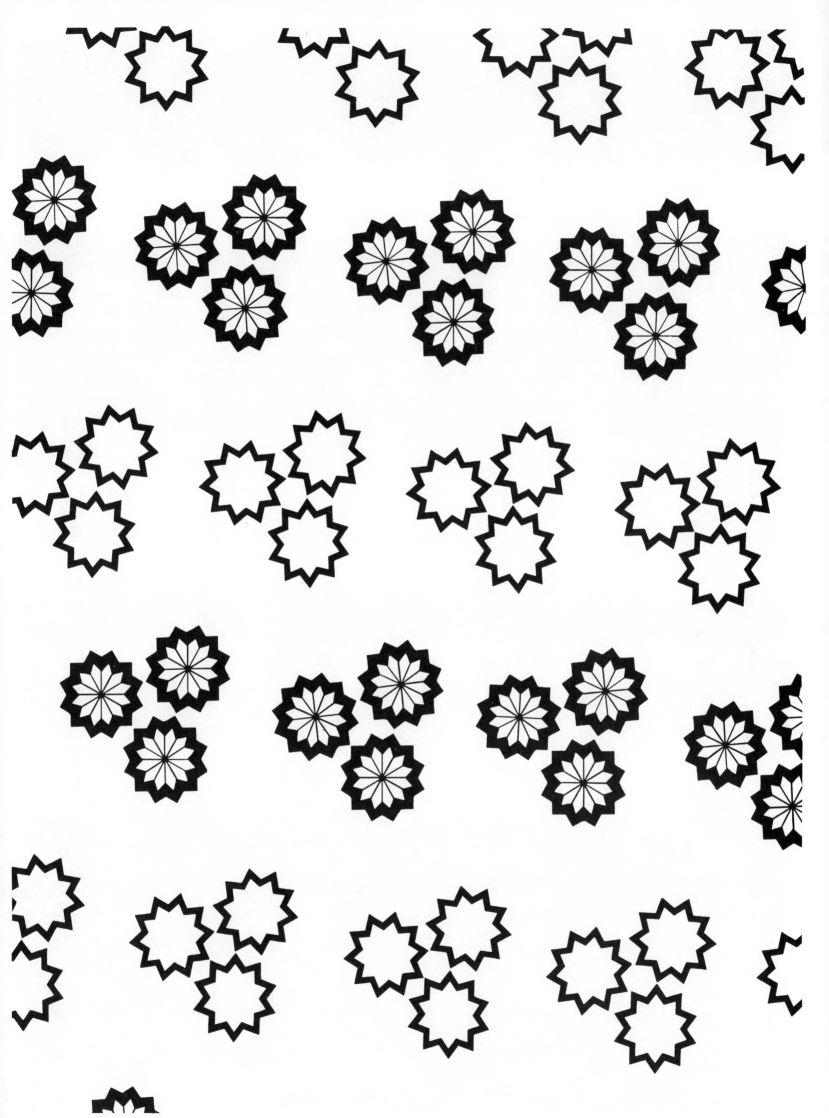

PLATE 67

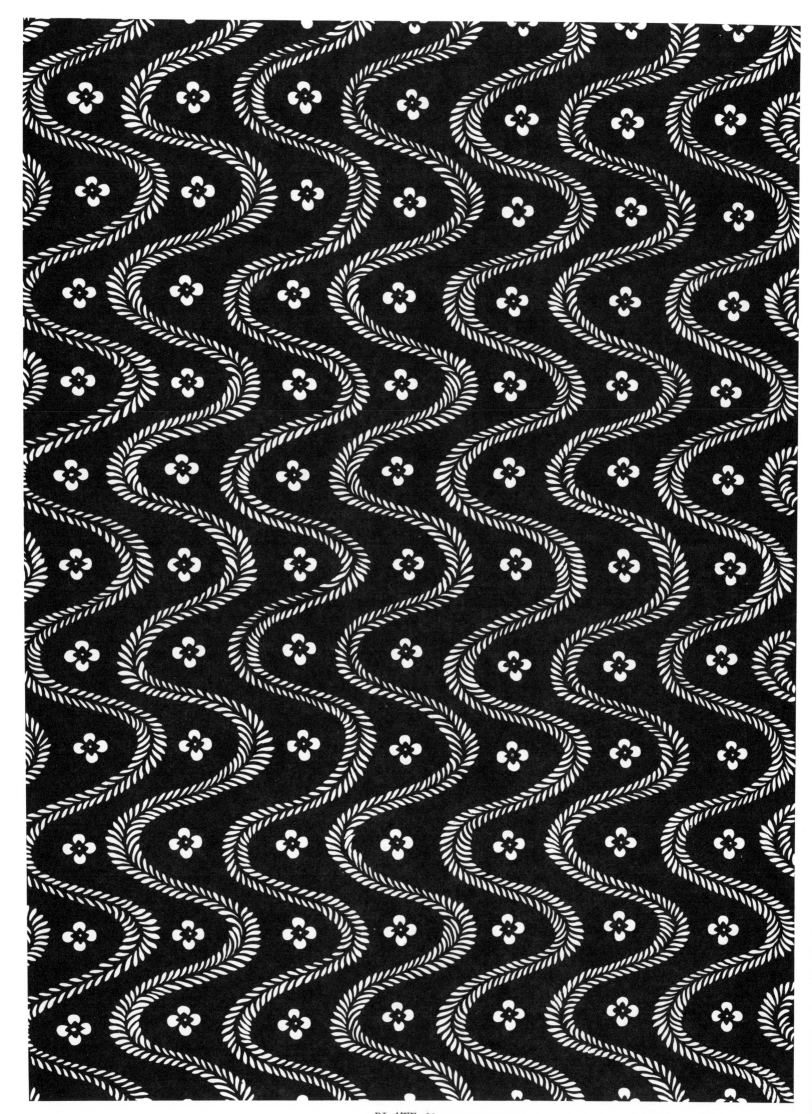

PLATE 68

PLATE 69

PLATE 70

PLATE 71

PLATE 72

PLATE 73

PLATE 74

PLATE 75

PLATE 76

PLATE 77

PLATE 78

PLATE 79

PLATE 80

PLATE 81

PLATE 82

PLATE 83

PLATE 84

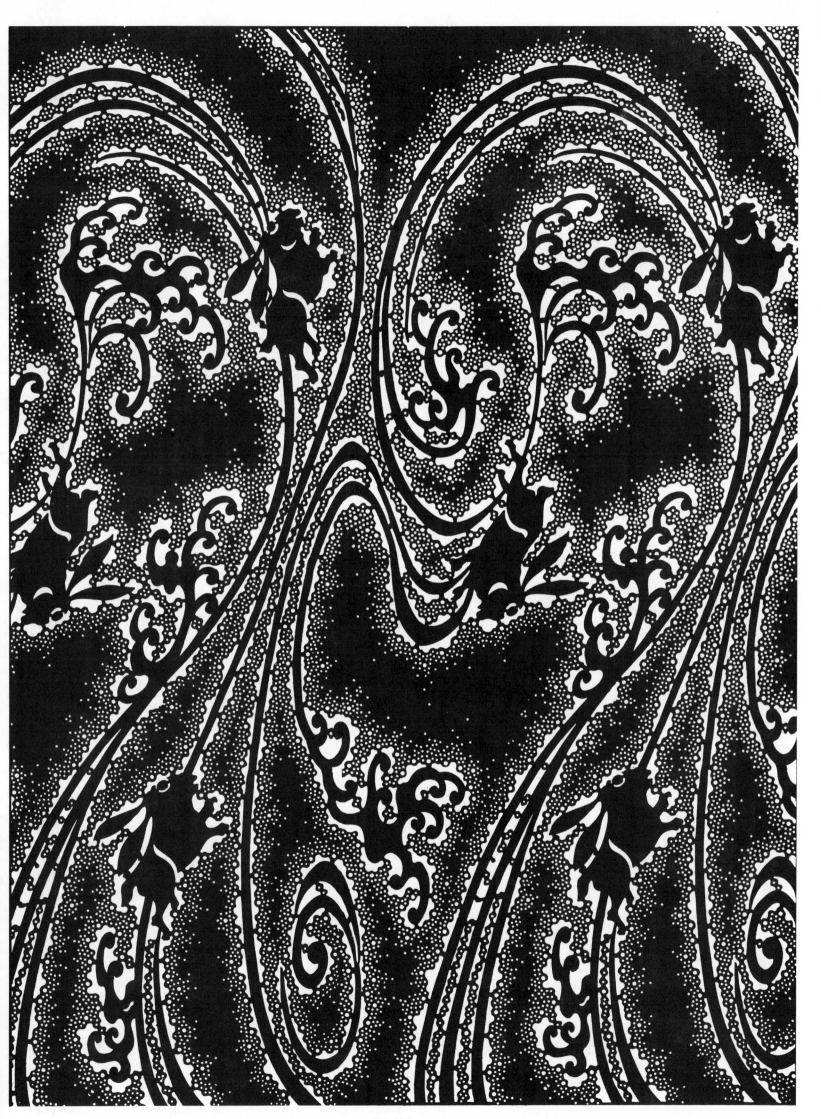

PLATE 85

PLATE 86

PLATE 87

PLATE 88